The bank robbery and other stories

A strange new friend page 3

The cricket boy page 4

That Jimbo page 15

Jack and the beanstalk page 33

The bank robbery page 47

Nelson

Thomas Nelson and Sons Ltd
Nelson House Mayfield Road
Walton-on-Thames Surrey
KT12 5PL UK

Thomas Nelson Australia
102 Dodds Street
South Melbourne
Victoria 3205 Australia

Nelson Canada
1120 Birchmount Road
Scarborough Ontario
M1K 5G4 Canada

Editorial Consultant: Donna Bailey
'A strange new friend' was written by Peggy Clulow and illustrated by Sara Silcoc'
'The cricket boy' was written by Sarah Tann and illustrated by Derek Collard
'That Jimbo' was written by Pamela Armstrong and illustrated by John Lobban
'Jack and the beanstalk' was written by Ron Deadman and illustrated by Tony Smith
'The bank robbery' was written by M. Morrin and illustrated by David Bryant

First published by Macmillan Education Ltd 1987

This edition published by Thomas Nelson and Sons Ltd 1992

I(T)P Thomas Nelson is an International Thomson Publishing Company

I(T)P is used under licence

ISBN 0-17-422533-4
NPN 9 8

Printed in China

A strange new friend

He sat in the corner just staring at me,
His eyes bright and shining and red as can be.
He had long pointed fingers and a green scaly skin,
And it gave me the shivers just looking at him.

But then I looked closer and to my surprise,
I noticed the monster had tears in his eyes.
He looked at me sadly and started to speak,
And the tears fell like rain down his green scaly cheek.

"Oh please don't be frightened," he sobbed through his
tears,
"I've wanted a playmate for so many years,
And then when I saw you this bright sunny day,
I hoped and I hoped that you wanted to play."

So, I sat down beside him and took his green hand
I'd made a new friend and the feeling was grand.
It's not what one looks like that counts in the end,
The real thing that matters is having a friend.

Peggy Clulow

The cricket boy

Long ago in the far away land of China
there lived a man called Hu.
He didn't like to work hard in the fields all day.
He just liked asking questions.
But to find the answers he had to think and
he had to read books.
Hu would ask,
"Why do small things grow big?"
"Why is the sun hot?"
"Why does the spring come after winter?"
All the people in the village thought he was very clever.

Hu had a son called Chang.
Chang did not like asking questions.
He didn't like thinking or reading.
What he liked best was to play with his crickets.
Hu was sad that his son didn't like asking questions.
So he said to himself, "If Chang doesn't want to learn to like books, then I must learn to like crickets."
So Hu would sit with Chang and together they would watch the crickets.
Soon Hu began to wonder, "Why do some crickets sing more loudly than others?"

Then he said,
"Why are some crickets so small?"
"Why are some crickets such brave fighters?"
And together Hu and Chang would watch
and talk and learn.
Soon they found a favourite cricket.
He was the best fighter of all.
Chang called him Black Dragon.
Chang's friends also had crickets.
Sometimes the boys would play cricket fights.
Black Dragon always won.
He was famous.

One day an important man came riding into the village on a white horse.

"Where is Chang?" he asked. "The Emperor of China wants to see him. He wants to see Black Dragon fight." Chang was very excited.

So Hu and Chang packed their bags and got ready to leave the very next day. When everything was ready Chang went to his room to fetch Black Dragon.

Black Dragon was resting in his jar.
Chang carefully lifted him up and walked towards the door.
He didn't see the mat. He tripped. The glass fell.
Black Dragon was dead.
Chang was so unhappy that he ran to the river and jumped in, hoping that he could also die.

Hu waited for his son.
When he did not come he went to his room and saw the broken jar.
He looked for Chang to try and comfort him.

Just then a fisherman came to the house.

"Look, Hu," he called, "I have found your son. He was in the river. He looks very ill."
Then Hu was very unhappy.
He quickly put Chang on the bed.
He thought his son was dead. He began to pray.

As he prayed a voice said to him, "Go to the gate and look behind the big stone."
Hu did as the voice told him.
There behind the big stone was a small cricket.
Gently he lifted it up in his hand.

"This must be a sign. I must take this cricket to the Emperor. I shall call it Bright Dragon."

When the Emperor saw Hu's small cricket, he laughed.

"How can a small cricket like that be a great fighter?" he said.

Then the fights began. Bright Dragon won every fight. After ten fights the Emperor said, "I give up. Your little cricket is so brave he wins every time. What would you like for a prize?"

Hu hung his head.

"There is only one thing I want," he said, "but you cannot give it to me."

The Emperor was very surprised.

"What is that?" he asked.

"All I want is for my son to be well again," said Hu.

"In that case you must go home at once," said the Emperor. "Go and look after him. I will give you some medicine to make him better."

So Hu started the long journey back again.
As soon as he was home he ran to his son's bed.
Chang lay quite still.

"My son," cried Hu. "Can you hear me?
Our little cricket won. He won every match.
The Emperor has sent you some medicine."
Just then Chang opened his eyes.
He looked at his father.

“Father,” he said, “I had such a strange dream.
I dreamt that I had to fight the great Emperor himself.
We fought ten times and I won every time.
Then the Emperor turned to me and said,
‘You are so brave that you can go home now.
Now I feel better, I shall get up.”

That night there was a party for the whole village.
Hu was so glad that his son was well again.
Everyone wanted to hear the story of the Emperor and how Bright Dragon had won the fight.

When everyone had at last gone to sleep,
Hu sat down and looked at the stars.
He wondered, “Why are they shining so brightly?
How did the little cricket win?
What really happened to Chang?”

But I don’t think that he will ever know
the answers to those questions.
Do you?

That Jimbo

Jimbo the dog lived with Mr and Mrs Jones and their children, Sue and Sam.
Jimbo was a little dog.
He had large floppy ears and a curly brown coat.
He always smiled happily and wagged his tail.
"This is my family. I am very happy," barked Jimbo.

He rolled in the grass. He chased hedgehogs. He barked at other dogs. He ran along the river bank. He visited the people next door. He played with the children in the street. He even swam in the goldfish pond!

"You are a bad dog, Jimbo," said Sue.

"You are a nice dog, Jimbo," said Sam. Jimbo jumped up and licked his face. They all had fun together.

In the summer holidays Anna came to stay.
Sue and Sam were her cousins.
Anna lived in another town far away.
She came in a plane by herself.
She was six years old.
Mr and Mrs Jones and Sue and Sam went to the airport to meet her.
Jimbo stayed at home.

"How nice to see you, Anna," said her aunt. She gave her a big hug. So did her uncle.

"We'll get your suitcase," said Sue and Sam. They liked having Anna to stay.

"When we get home, you can play with Jimbo," said Sue.

Jimbo? Anna stood still.
She had forgotten that her cousins had a dog.

Anna was afraid of dogs.
Dogs looked big and fierce. She did not like dogs.
She loved Toto, her cat. She loved Tom, her bird.
But she was not sure that she would love Jimbo.
Anna was very quiet on the way home from
the airport.
Soon they arrived at Sam and Sue's house.

Jimbo was very pleased to see his family again. He shook with delight. His ears stood up stiffly. A big welcoming grin was on his face.

"Here they come," he said to himself. "I will give them my loudest bark. **Woof, woof**."

Anna did not like Jimbo's bark at all.
"Oh dear," she thought. "That Jimbo sounds very fierce."
"Everyone get out of the car," called her uncle. "We're home."
Jimbo jumped up at the car window.
Anna looked at him as she got out of the car and walked inside with her uncle.
"That girl has brown eyes just like mine," thought Jimbo.
He loved Anna from that moment.
"Don't be afraid of Jimbo," said her aunt to Anna. "He likes you. Really he does."

Anna felt safe once she was in the house. But poor Jimbo was sad. His ears drooped. He wagged his tail slowly. He wanted Anna to play with him. He wanted her to be his special friend.

The next day Sue and Sam went outside to play with Anna. Jimbo was very happy to see them. He ran around. He jumped up and down. Anna tried hard not to be afraid. She stayed close to Sam and Sue.

Jimbo is nice in so many ways, thought Anna to herself.
He is always smiling. He has lovely brown hair.
He has big brown eyes. He is very friendly.
But he seems so big.
He wants to jump up and lick my face and he barks very loudly.

Sam ran to the back door and took down Jimbo's lead from its hook.

"Come on, Anna," he said cheerfully, "I'm taking Jimbo for a walk.
We will take him on his lead.
He won't jump up. He won't bark."

Anna held Sam's hand very tightly.
They all walked along the street.
Jimbo thought happily, "I like going for walks with Anna and Sam."

"Would you like to hold Jimbo's lead?" Sam asked Anna.
"I will hold your hand. Don't be afraid."

So Anna held Sam's hand and with her other hand she held Jimbo's lead. She felt very brave. Suddenly she felt happy also.

Jimbo also felt happy. He thought, "I will turn round and thank Anna for being my friend."

As they walked along he suddenly stopped and looked back at Anna.

"Thank you, Anna," he barked. "Woof, woof."
Anna had a fright.
Sam had to stop her from running away.

"Never mind, Anna," he said.
"You will soon like Jimbo."

They went home and the children went inside for their tea.
Jimbo trotted away. He was feeling happy.
He had enjoyed his walk with Anna and Sam.
He felt like running and jumping.
He raced round the house. He chased the cat.
He picked up a stick in his sharp teeth.
He ran round and round with it.

Suddenly he saw a big box on the grass.
"I will jump over that box," he thought.
Too late!
The stick caught on the box as he jumped.
His back leg hit the box. A pain shot through it.
Poor Jimbo. He limped to the front door.
"Help me! I have hurt myself," he barked.
Nobody heard him. Nobody came.

Anna finished her tea.

"May I go outside and play?" she asked.

"Of course you may," said her aunt.

Anna ran out of the front door.
She did not know that Jimbo was there.

"Oh," she cried. Then she stopped.
What was wrong with Jimbo?
Jimbo was not barking. Jimbo was not jumping.
Anna saw that Jimbo was limping.

Suddenly Anna was not afraid of Jimbo.

"Jimbo," she said, and she bent down by the little dog. "Don't worry, Jimbo," she whispered. "I'll go and get help."

"Aunt, aunt," she called. "Jimbo has hurt his leg. Please come quickly."

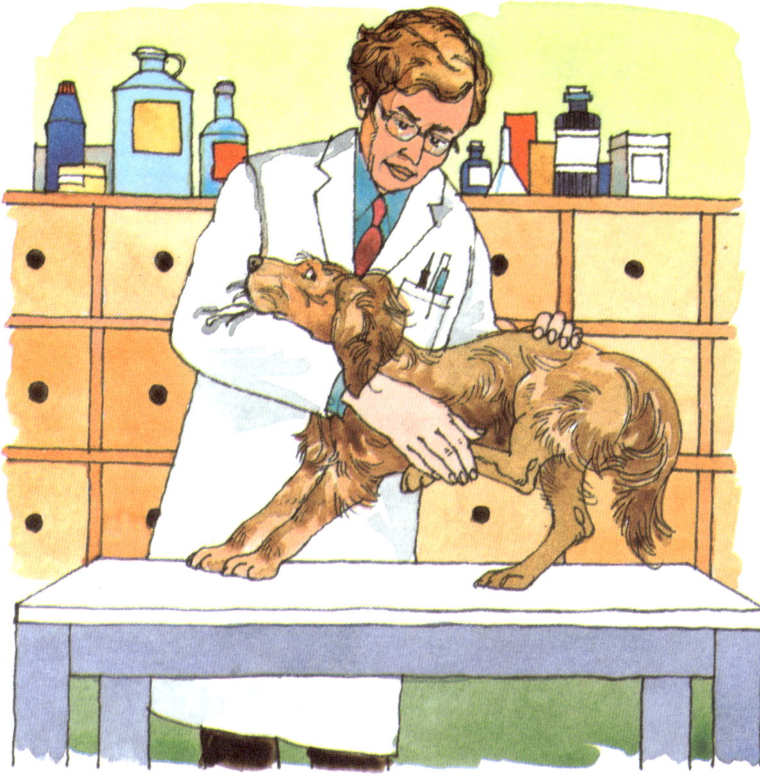

Everyone ran outside.
Her aunt picked up Jimbo very carefully.
Uncle drove them all in the car to see the vet.
The vet felt Jimbo's leg gently.

"He has hurt a muscle," he said. "I will put a bandage on it."

"I'm glad Jimbo is not badly hurt," said Anna.

"So are we," said Sue and Sam.

"So are we," said her aunt and uncle.

Jimbo was looked after until his leg was strong again.
Who took care of Jimbo?
Who was the happiest when Jimbo was better?
Why, Anna of course.

Jack and the beanstalk

Once upon a time, there was a boy called Jack.
He lived with his mother who was a poor widow.
One day, when they had no money for food,
Jack's mother sent him to market to sell their cow.
But Jack came home with no cow and with no money.

What had happened?

"I gave the cow to an old woman I met," said Jack, "and she gave me these."

He showed his mother five beans.

"These are magic beans," he said.

"**Fool, idiot,**" cried his mother. "You are a stupid boy, Jack."

She picked up the beans and threw them out of the window. Poor Jack went sadly into the garden.

The next morning he looked out of the window, and what did he see? He saw a tall twisty bean stalk which had grown so much in the night that it reached right up to the sky.

Well it looked so easy to climb that
Jack decided to see if he could get to the top.
Up and up he went – right up into the clouds.
At the top he found a long rough road.

Suddenly he came face to face with
the old woman who had given him the magic beans.
"Jack," she said, "be careful.
Somewhere along this road lives a
giant – a wicked giant that killed your father."
Jack was angry, "Where is he?" he asked.
But the old woman would not tell him.

So Jack went on.
Soon he came to a great, tall house.
On the doorstep waiting for him was a very tall woman.
"Go away, boy," she said.
"My husband, the terrible giant, will soon be home.
He will gobble you up for his supper."
Too late, too late.

Thud, Thud, Thud. It was the giant coming home and making the earth tremble with every step.

"Quick, boy," said the giant's wife. "Hide in the oven."

So Jack jumped into the oven and watched the terrible giant filling his mouth with the huge pieces of bread and meat his wife had given him for supper.

When he had finished he told his wife
to bring him all his gold.
Jack watched him grinning greedily as
the giant counted each coin.
"All mine, all mine," said the giant.
Then he told his wife to bring him his magic hen.
Jack watched amazed as the magic hen
laid a golden egg every time the giant told it to.

But then the wicked giant growled,
"Fee-fi-foxy-foy
I smell the blood of
A naughty boy."
"Don't be silly," said his wife.
So the giant grunted and went to sleep.

Jack heard him snoring so loudly that the house shook.
So he jumped out of the oven and grabbed the bag of gold and the magic hen.
He ran as fast as his legs would carry him until he reached the beanstalk.
He dropped the gold and the magic hen and climbed down.

Jack's mother was very happy now.
Her son had brought home a bag full of
gold coins and a magic hen!
Now they could buy food and a cow to give them milk.
But Jack wasn't happy.
He could not forget the wicked giant who
had killed his father.
So early one morning ...

Early one morning he climbed the tall twisty beanstalk again, and made his way along the road to the wicked giant's house.

He climbed through an open window and hid under a table.

Suddenly, **thud, thud, thud, crash, bang.**

The giant was home.

Slurp, slurp, gobble gobble.

That was the giant eating his supper.

Then the giant began playing with his magic harp.
This sang sweet songs to him.
But suddenly the giant put down his harp and said,

"Fe-fi-foxy-foy
I smell the blood of
A naughty boy."

But he couldn't see Jack, so he fell asleep.

And what did Jack do then?
He crawled out, put the magic harp under his arm and ran as fast as his legs could carry him towards the beanstalk.

But the magic harp called out, "Help, master, help."
The giant woke up and chased Jack along the road.
But Jack just reached the beanstalk.
He clambered down with the terrible wicked giant huffing and puffing behind him.

"Stop, grrr, stop!" bellowed the giant.
"I'll catch you and eat you for breakfast."
But Jack had reached the bottom of the beanstalk by now. There he saw an axe.
What did he do?

There was only one thing he could do.
He picked up the axe and chopped down the beanstalk. **Crash. Bang. Wallop!**
The giant fell to the ground with a terrible thud.
Jack smiled.
The giant was dead.

The bank robbery

Ben and Katy will never forget the day of the bank robbery.
They were walking home from school along the High Street.
They were talking about the television programme they were going to watch when they got home.
The High Street was very quiet.
Usually it was busy with adults doing their shopping and with children running home from school.
But today was different.
Today something was wrong.

Outside the bank was a large red car.
The engine was running and smoke was coming out of the exhaust.
A man was sitting in the driving seat of the car.
He looked very nervous and kept staring at the front of the bank.
He did not turn the car engine off.
He kept looking at the bank.
He must have been waiting for someone to come out of the bank.

Ben and Katy looked at each other.
"He looks very odd to me," said Ben.
"Yes he does," said Katy. "Do you think we should tell someone?"
"Perhaps we should telephone the police instead," said Ben.
"Let me try to remember the number of the car first," said Katy.

Before the children could do anything,
two men burst through the door of the bank.
They were each clutching a large brown canvas bag.
As soon as the driver of the car saw them,
he flung open the back of the car.
The two men ran towards the car.

They threw their canvas bags on to the back seat and jumped in themselves.
Then the car roared away from the kerb.
Within seconds the robbers and their car had gone.
Ben and Katy stared at each other in amazement.
Had they really seen a robbery?
They looked towards the bank but they were too frightened to do anything.
No one else seemed to have seen the robbery.

The High Street had been so quiet but
then the street seemed to get busy again.
Everyone was rushing about as usual.
Suddenly the bank's burglar alarm began to ring loudly.
A few people stopped and stared at the bank but
then they walked on.
They thought it was a false alarm.

The sound of police sirens could be heard in the distance.
People in the High Street stopped.
They looked at the bank and listened to the burglar alarm.
Then they carried on rushing about as usual.
A few minutes later Ben and Katy saw a car racing up the High Street.
It wasn't a police car. It was the robbers' car.
It was coming back!

As the robbers reached the bank, the driver slammed on the car brakes.
The car skidded and swerved, then it disappeared through the park gates and into the park next to the bank.

"Did you see that?" cried Ben. "Was it really them?"

“Yes, I’m sure it was,” said Katy.

“They must have heard the police car coming so they turned back up the High Street,” said Ben.

“Now they’re hiding in the park,” said Katy.

“What a silly place to hide,” said Ben. “There’s only one way in and out of the park.”

Within seconds the sound of another car could be heard speeding up the High Street.
This time it was the police car.
It came to a halt in front of the bank.
A tall policeman sitting in the passenger seat jumped out of the car and ran into the bank.

"Now is our chance," said Ben. "Let's go and tell the policeman driving the car what we have seen."

"And we can tell him where the robbers are hiding," said Katy.

Before they could reach the police car, the policeman had returned and the car raced down the road right past the park.

"What are we going to do now?" asked Katy.

"I'm not sure," said Ben. "You watch the park gates while I go and tell the bank manager."

Katy stood guard as Ben walked into the bank. Just inside the door Ben met the bank guard.

"Where do you think you're going, son?" asked the guard.

"I'd like to see the bank manager," said Ben.

"I'm afraid he's very busy at the moment," said the guard. "There has just been a robbery."

"Yes, I know," said Ben. "The robbers are in the park."

“Oh yes!” said the guard. “You’ll be telling me next they’re having a picnic!”

“But they **are** in the park,” shouted Ben.
He explained everything that he and Katy had seen.
At first the guard did not believe Ben.
When he described the robbers in detail, the guard began to listen more carefully.

Soon the guard realised that Ben was telling the truth.
He took him to see the bank manager who listened to the whole story.

"Well done, Ben," said the manager. "I'll telephone the police at once and give them the car number."
He smiled and picked up the phone.
As soon as he had spoken to the police he asked the others to follow him to the park gates.

Katy was still there.

"Are they still in the park?" shouted Ben.

"Yes they are," said Katy.

Suddenly they heard the sound of a car in the park. It was travelling very quickly towards the gates. Seconds later the robbers' car raced through the gates. They all watched as the car went down the road in the same direction as the police car had gone!

"Oh goodness," said Ben. "What do we do now?"

"Never mind," said the bank manager. "The police have got their number. They will soon catch them."

Just at that moment they all heard
the screeching of car tyres.
They looked down the road in time to see the robbers' car swerve to avoid running into the police car.

The robbers' car crashed into the kerb.
The two policemen jumped out of their car and rushed towards the robbers' car.
They pulled the robbers out of their car and handcuffed them.
Then they drove them off towards the police station.

Ben and Katy could not wait to get home to tell their mother what had happened. Their mother listened for a few minutes and then she smiled.

"Oh yes," she said, "very interesting indeed. Now tell me what you did at school today."

"Never mind what we did at school today," said Ben. "We know what we are going to write about tomorrow."